THE BEGINNER'S GUIDE TO TEACHING ENGLISH ONLINE

This book is dedicated to

Charlene & Rick

Thank you

Table of Contents

INTRODUCTION

The term lingua franca refers to the language used between people who do not share a native language. It is also known as a world language. People have been using lingua franca since Greco-Roman times. Latin and Greek being the two most influential languages of the age. They were used as the standard for communication across the roman empire. Literature, mathematics, science and philosophy were written in these international languages.

The exciting thing about lingua franca is that it's always changing. Although Latin and Greek had a tremendous influence on the English language, they are no longer the current lingua franca we use to communicate. As empires and dynasties rise and fall, so do the ways in which we communicate.

It is also important to note that the lingua franca is very different depending on which continent you're on. Geography plays a vital role in how we speak. Classical Chinese was the lingua franca in East Asia for many centuries before it was replaced in the 20th century by a contemporary form of written Chinese.

In the African continent before french colonization there were many different lingua francas depending on the region. Afrikaans being the most notable one in South Africa. Before Columbus "discovered" North America and brought with him European languages, there were many different indigenous languages spoken. Many of which are now extinct and forgotten due to European colonization. The point is, before the digital age, and mass globalization occurred, lingua franca was defined largely by geography and which continent you were on.

Today we have the internet, and we have access to people across the world from the comfort of our living rooms. The lingua franca of today is English. It is the international language of business, science, mathematics, and everything in between. Scores of people from around the world clamour to find affordable, quick and straightforward ways to learn English. So they too might engage this new global digital market. As half the websites on the internet are in English, the need for English proficiency has grown to adapt to this market.

This is where people like you come in. Demand for English teachers has risen in the last decade to keep up with the global economy. In places like China, UAE, Japan,

India and Brazil where economies have skyrocketed with the birth of the digital age, so has the demand for English. English teachers are sought after across the globe to accommodate this growing need.

In China where the population is fast approaching 1.5 billion people, English proficiency has become a requirement for kids hoping to get into university and later a good job. Middle-class families hoping to give their children the best hope of getting into good schools are exposing their children to English as newborns. In cities throughout China English preschools, daycares and afterschool programs are prevalent on every block. The English craze is in full swing.

The effect it has had on English speaking countries such as Canada, USA, UK, Australia and South Africa is that more and more people are being enticed into moving abroad to foreign countries to start their journeys as ESL teachers (English as a second language) myself included.

In the spring of 2016 a month before my graduation from university, I was stuck. I found myself without any real direction. I was about to graduate with a degree in History and had no idea what I wanted to do with it. In North American culture university and college is the expected next step for young adults leaving high school. So naturally after high school I chose the only thing that interested me, history.

After spending four wonderful years at Laurentian University in Sudbury, Ontario a place where I gained friendships to last a lifetime. I was stumped about my next steps, I knew I didn't want to pursue a career as a historian and I didn't necessarily want to become a history teacher either. What I wanted more than anything after spending my life in school was to travel, but how could I sustainably do that full time? A month before the end of my final fourth-year exams, I found the answer! While researching long term travel, I came across teaching english as a foreign language. I was hooked. After my last exam I enrolled myself in a TEFL course being offered in my hometown.

A month later and my bank account a thousand dollars lighter I was certified to teach English as an international ESL teacher. It's important to mention that, not every ESL teacher has a TEFL certificate, and I've certainly met teachers who didn't have this certification. I personally found this certification helpful as at the end of the program there was a placement aspect that helped to connect me with my first ESL job in Guangzhou, China. I went with a top-rated TEFL teacher training company in Canada (Oxfordseminars.ca). They were a bit expensive and a lot more costly than I was expecting, but after a month of in-class training seminars and the lifetime placement program following the final exam, I considered it to be a necessary expense.

A week after finishing the courses and obtaining the

certificate, I was on a plane with my friend to Madagascar on a volunteer trip we had been planning for months where I would get to use my TEFL certificate first hand. After a missed flight in Toronto and two extra flights to make up for the original missed flight, It took us nearly a week to arrive in Madagascar. Toronto to Las Vegas to Houston to Paris to Antananarivo, and then 24 hours on a bus packed tight with 12 other locals, and finally, a quick boat ride to the small island of Nosy Komba.

This island is where I officially started my ESL journey. I'd initially went to Madagascar to take part in a month-long forest conservation project that would help to assist in monitoring the local wildlife indigenous to Madagascar. Once getting there, I volunteered to help teach ESL classes in some of the local villages, as well as continuing to help with the forest conservation project.

I remember tagging, along with one of the resident ESL teachers to study and see how she taught her classes. I'll never forget that first class, It was a scorching hot day, coupled with my rising anxiety meant that I had already sweated through my shirt tenfold before I'd entered the classroom. The class was a mixed bag of ages, the youngest being a two year old girl who was being babysat by her sister to an older man in his late seventies sitting at the front of the classroom. The class was learning at a basic beginner level, the lesson that day was numbers one to ten and colours.

I spent the next month going to this local village twice a week and fumbling my way through different ways to teach this class. I'll tell you now, I wasn't any good, I lacked confidence and I struggled to find ways to control this rowdy group of kids and adults. The language barrier felt larger every class I went to. The adult class I sat in on was a little better and a particularly memorable class included trying to translate Kanye West songs. My first experience teaching English was shaky at best but I was determined to educate myself on more effective ways to teach and maintain control in the classroom.

As I sat in the crowded international terminal in Antananarivo, I told myself that no one is good at anything on their first try, so don't give up on this. Three months later I was stepping off the train in Guangzhou, China. I taught English in Guangzhou for eight months. My time in China was terrifying, confusing, frustrating and a serious lesson in patience to say the least, but it was where I first learned about the ESL craze and how profitable it could be for English speakers.

It was there in Guangzhou where I learned the skills to maintain control in a classroom, and how to use TPR (total physical response). I learnt how to engage young learners in English games, sentence structure, phonics, reading tricks and much more.

The beginning of my stay was difficult, learning how to teach as well as navigating Chinese work culture. This coupled with the nagging homesickness made for a rough couple of months. Towards the end of my contract I felt more than ready to say goodbye to China but not as ready to say goodbye to my students, the friends I made and teaching ESL.

This led me to the world of teaching ESL Online.

In this book I hope to answer some critical questions you have about starting a career as an online English teacher.

- Teaching online vs. teaching abroad

- Different online companies vs. Freelancing

- Applying and Interviewing

- Essential equipment and useful rewards

- Improving your "classroom"

- TPR tips and tricks

- Resources

CHAPTER 1

<u>Teaching Abroad vs Teaching Online</u>

This chapter will cover some of the significant differences between teaching online vs. teaching abroad and discovering which one is right for you. When it comes to teaching ESL choosing the perfect 'Classroom' whether it be in a different country or from the comfort of your living room is essential in determining your success.

When I was finishing my TEFL certificate, I didn't know about online teaching and the entire community of people who choose to work from their homes teaching English. I'm not sure if I would have chosen that route instead of moving abroad but knowing all the options is always reassuring when starting a new career.

<u>Teaching Abroad</u>

First, let me say that it was my love of travel that moved me to leave home and teach abroad. The idea of living and working in a different country opened my mind to the various opportunities available. I was brimming with excitement at the possibility of exploring new cities, mountain trekking and museum browsing. The teaching for me was a means to an end, a way for me to support myself while exploring. Though teaching wasn't the primary motivator for me to move abroad, it did teach me valuable skills I was able to apply to my online business as an ESL teacher.

If you are thinking about teaching abroad, here are some things to consider. Although most countries are looking to employ English teachers not all countries are willing to pay you the salary you are probably used to. The minimum wage is very different in Thailand than it is in Canada or the US. So, if a high pay cheque is a priority for you, then you'll have to do your research on who and what country to work in.

Currently, the highest paying countries for TEFL certified teachers are China, South Korea, Japan and UAE. These are not the only high paying countries, but they do pay above average. Salary is also going to depend on the experience, certifications, and the demo interview you present to new employers.

Location is going to be a significant consideration when choosing a school. Big cities such as Beijing,

Shanghai, Guangzhou, Tokyo, and Dubai tend to attract more expats and have more modern conveniences like good wifi, local transportation, nightlife, gyms, movie theatres and restaurants. It will also be easier to find other people in the same situation as yourself living and working abroad. The need for ESL teachers has been steadily on the rise for years, and the search for dedicated, outgoing and enthusiastic teachers is ongoing. If this is your first time living abroad, it might be easier to move to one of these bigger cities, especially if you don't speak the local language.

There are opportunities to teach in more rural areas outside the main travel hubs, but be warned it'll be more of a culture shock and you'll have to go without many of the conveniences your used to. This being said, living and working in a small town can be very rewarding, and you will no doubt get a more authentic experience. Living outside the major cities offers you a chance to become a bigger part of the community, forces you to learn the language, and try local food. In many of these towns and villages, it will be more of a rarity to see foreigners and people will be very curious to get to know you.

In smaller communities, be prepared for larger class sizes, the schools will want to take advantage of the opportunity to expose as many students as possible to a native English speaker. There are many positions available in larger cities, this usually means the salary tends to be higher than schools with smaller budgets. If you want to live in a smaller town than you will have to shop around and negotiate for a higher salary.

Wherever you choose to work, ask the school to arrange for someone to help you with getting settled. Trust me, setting up a bank account and getting a phone plan in China when you don't speak Mandarin is a serious test in patience. From getting an apartment to figuring out the local bus routes many tasks can seem impossible without help, don't be afraid to reach out to your school for support.

Finally, you have to consider the different work culture mentality. I know in Canada there are many different cultures and people who live there come from all over the globe. Work culture in Canada means to be accepting of all different kinds of people and be able to work and communicate with people of different religions, race, beliefs, gender, sexuality, and disabilities. This work culture will not be the same in many parts of the world. When researching places to live and work, you have to remember that different countries have different values and expectations.

Western women looking to work in the UAE will find life dramatically different than the ones they were used to in North America or Europe. Qualified non-white teachers looking for work in China or Japan will have a harder time finding a job then white high school graduates. LGBQT individuals should not look for work in certain parts of South America/Middle East/Africa as it is still illegal in many countries.

Do your research.

Teaching Online

Teaching English online was a very foreign concept for me in the beginning. When I started researching, I had many questions about classroom management, connecting to students and class schedules. As I kept looking, I was able to discover whole communities of ESL teachers on different social media platforms (mostly Facebook) that were connecting and helping each other with common problems they encountered in their classrooms.

Most online ESL classrooms have similar platforms to each other. There is course material on one half of the screen, and on the other half are the teacher and students. The teacher and students can see each other and the course material. The teacher controls the materials and functions of the classroom. The teacher is the one in control of the lesson management, they are the ones who control when to move onto the next page, and if the student can click or draw on the screen. Online ESL classrooms usually have an interactive aspect to the lesson where the students can click on the correct answers or draw on the screen. There is usually a text box on the screen with a translation function for the teacher and students to use to communicate with each other.

I'm not very tech capable, I know how to start a word document and open facebook. So before I started teaching online, I was worried I wouldn't be able to operate the teaching platform. When I started working at my first ESL company, I was pleased to learn it wasn't that tricky to figure out. The company made me go through a training week where I learned how to use the different features, and I had to practise lessons with other teachers. So don't be worried about the tech aspect of the job, you will go through a company training process to learn how to control the platform.

It's important to remember, each company is different and has unique procedures, rules and ways of assigning students to teachers. Some companies assign you students based on teacher performance, and other companies let students choose their own teachers.

The first company I worked for let students choose their own teachers based on short 30-second introduction videos the teachers created. This gave students a chance to get to know their teacher before they started class. After the lesson, students were encouraged to leave 'stars' by their favourite teachers so that they were able to book them again in the future. The more 'stars' a teacher had, the more eligible they became for promotions/pay raises. This is one example of how one particular ESL company ran its program. There are many variations of pay structures and student allocation.

At first when I was first hired, I waited two weeks before I had my first class. I was teaching pretty regularly three weeks after I had been launched as an official teacher at the company. Depending on which company you are hired with is going to determine the times you teach. The company I worked for was based in China and only offered their program to Chinese students ages 3 to 18. Due to the time difference between Toronto, Canada, and Beijing, China the times I taught at were between four to nine am, I only had a 5-hour window of teaching time each day.

In China, because there is such competition between students to stand out, there is a push for kids to learn English at a young age; so many times, they will go to after school Engligh programs either online or in person. The online classes offer parents a cheaper way to put their kids in English class. And because of this, many parents turn to the online alternative but the majority of classes are held Monday to Friday after school from four to nine at night, which is usually the North American morning.

The best part of teaching so early is that by the time you've finished classes, everyone else is just waking up. Being able to finish work by 9 am gives you the freedom to pursue all those hobbies you never seemed to have time for.

Whether you teach online or abroad, there are many aspects of the job to consider. You ultimately have to decide which one you will be best suited for. Are you the type of person that doesn't have a lot of commitments that will make moving a problem for you. Do you like to explore new cities and eat different food? Are you comfortable living away from family and friends and potentially missing significant milestones in their lives? People don't generally celebrate Christmas in China, so I worked a full 8-hour shift teaching my regular classes on Christmas day. Moments like this can make living abroad difficult for a lot of people. If you are the type of person who has too many obligations to leave home, but still wants to experience a new culture and work as an ESL teacher, then you might be better suited for online teaching.

Finding a way to teach ESL from my home and continuing to develop new skills as an educator was one of the many reasons I turned to online teaching. I hope you figure out the best teaching platform for yourself either online or abroad, good luck.

CHAPTER 2

Established Companies vs Freelance

There are many options available to you when you decide to teach ESL online. You can either work as a teacher at an established company, or you can go off on your own and start a freelance career. There are pros and cons to both and there are many people who start their ESL career teaching for a company and later do freelance work.

Established Company

Many people who teach online have at one point started off teaching for another company. There are many ESL companies online, and they are always looking for personable and engaging teachers to join their company.

One of the many benefits of working for an established

company is that they already have a student base. This means you won't have to go through the trouble of getting and keeping students. Although some companies let their students choose their own teachers, so in those cases you do have to think about retaining students. The larger the company, the bigger student base they will have, but they will also have more teachers, which means more competition.

The curriculum you teach is another huge consideration. Generally you will be following a standard company curriculum. The level of freedom in what and how you teach will depend on the company. Some places will be more flexible in how you teach, and if you feel that the lesson material is too difficult or easy, then you might have more freedom to change the lesson to fit the student.

Most companies will test the students to place them in the appropriate learning level before they assign them a teacher. These tests are not always accurate because most students learn to read and write English in schools but rarely get to practise spoken English. This makes placing students in the appropriate levels difficult. Often, when I'm teaching I have to change my lesson to engage the students in speaking more.

Most lessons will have a theme and a corresponding vocabulary to fit the lesson, getting students to understand the vocabulary and use it in conversation is usually the goal of the class. The negatives of working for an established company is that often, the theme, vocabulary and activities of the class are set by the company. You can change them in small ways to fit the student, but ultimately if you think the material is too advanced or easy, you can't move them from their current learning level. Those higher up decisions are for the parents and the company to decide. You will have less authority in decisions than if you were with a smaller company, or if you were to freelance.

Pay is always a huge factor when your choosing where to work. Many companies pay through third-party websites like PayPal, which I find is more convenient than setting up through a bank. You can also have them direct deposit money to your bank account; this is usually a longer process and needs more documentation. Each company will have a different pay schedule, and some will pay every week others every month.

The first company I worked for paid out on the 12th of every month, but most times it arrived earlier on the 3rd. One of the biggest concerns I hear from people looking to start teaching online is that they might not get paid for teaching. This is a valid concern, especially when you are receiving money from a source online. This is why it's essential to research the company you want to work for, but keep in mind no company would be able to retain teachers if they didn't pay them.

Many companies are based in China or different parts of Asia so finding information on them is more complicated. I have found that Facebook seems to be an excellent place to look for company reviews. Many companies have facebook groups for their teachers to talk to each other about lessons, share tips about student behavior problems and tech issues. Try reaching out to these groups and asking people what they have to say about the company. Most teachers are more than eager to help new teachers getting started and pretty candid about the realities of the company.

The average pay for an hour class is 18-20 USD or 23.50-26 CAD. Anything less than this isn't worth your time, and I would be cautious of any company offering more than this without previous work experience. It's important to remember that many companies will advertise "up to $20/hour" this is different than "starting at $20/hour." Many companies have incentive programs for you to make more money, if your students re-sign after their contract is finished, sometimes you make a commission off that student. When companies advertise looking for teachers, make sure they are not adding this incentive program as part of your salary.

When talking to potential employers, be clear about your base pay. Base pay is the amount you get paid per class taught, whether that's per hour or half hour is based on the company.

Most companies hire teachers as independent contractors for a fixed time period of either six months to a year. The contracts they ask you to sign are basic, and they go over appropriate student teacher relationships, pay rate, sick days, missed class penalties and other company policies. Some companies have a probation period where if they don't like how you teach, they let you go after a month.

When you interview with a company you let them know your availability, usually they want a Monday to Friday 17:00 to 21:00 Beijing time commitment, which translates to 5 to 9 am Eastern Standard time.

There are many different online ESL markets, and the largest one is the Asian audience. When turning to online classrooms, students usually want to be taught by native English speakers and will pay decent money for this experience. Students also generally want to be taught by teachers with neutral accents. South African teachers sometimes find it difficult to find employers willing to hire them because of their unique accents. This is the same for people from the UK and Australia. Canadians and Americans tend to have an easier time finding jobs online than others because of their more neutral accents. This does not mean that there is no opportunity for people from these countries only that you will have to look for a company that accepts these accents.

You have to consider many factors when looking for an ESL company, but the good news is that the internet has an endless supply of resources to help you find the best fit for yourself. If working for someone else is not what your interested in doing and you're looking to branch out on your own then maybe freelance is best for you.

Freelance ESL Teacher

As a freelance ESL teacher, you will have a laundry list of work to do, and it can seem overwhelming in the beginning. Before you start advertising your services, sit down and make a list of what you want to specialize in. If you make yourself available to teach many different subjects, ages and levels too early into your freelancing career, you run the risk of burning yourself out. You would be better to specialize in the beginning and get a handle on what you are doing, then offer more services as your student base grows.

For example, advertising your services in beginners business English to university students will attract more attention then if you were to advertise conversational English classes to all ages and levels. This will also make it easier to create and perfect the lessons you want to teach and build a stronger curriculum.

Once you've chosen your target students and developed an initial curriculum, you'll have to decide on what platform you'll teach through. Skype is a popular choice for many ESL freelancers. You'll also want to get set up a website to legitimize yourself and promote your unique personality and skills that will make you the right choice for potential students. Also, it is worth looking into getting certifications to such as TEFL/

TESL which you can get online.

Then focus your energy on promoting your website on different social media profiles such as Facebook, Twitter, Instagram, I've personally found Facebook groups to be the most popular place to get new students. Don't underestimate the importance of advertising at your local cafe's, cultural centres, markets, gyms and libraries, most places where you know international students, and people hang out.

Starting out as a freelancer will be challenging throughout the entire process because you'll continuously have to be looking for students and ways to stand out against the competition. This means that money will always be uncertain, but you'll be your own boss and get to set your own price. Most ESL companies offer deals for the first class to see if the student wants to continue, many offer one class as a free trial but I don't recommend this in the beginning as you might end up providing more free classes then paid ones. Although offering some type of first class promotion would be a smart way to entice students to try your class and see if they like you without committing to a class package.

Pricing your classes appropriately early on is vital because if you raise the prices of your classes as you start to become more established, you run the risk of losing loyal students. Average classes cost around $30 to $40 for general classes and $50 to $60 for more specialized classes. You can also charge special prices for class packages such as $250 for ten classes. Group classes where you teach more than one student at once is another popular option as it gives the students a chance to practise their English with more people. Create a clear price list for potential students, including all promotions.

It will be challenging to start as a freelancer but not impossible, if your willing to put in the time to create good material, focus on student satisfaction and be willing to spend money on advertising engaging campaigns then you will be successful. You won't be successful overnight, but consistency and persistence is going to be the name of the game.

CHAPTER 3

Applying and Interviewing

When your applying to reputable ESL companies the time between the application and interview to being launched as a teacher can be two weeks to a month. Every company has its own process, but it can be a series of interviews and demonstrations/demos before you teach your first class.

Application Process

I briefly mentioned in chapter 2, the importance of researching the companies you want to work for. Look at each company's career page, and you can find these on different Facebook groups like 'online ESL teachers,' 'online ESL teacher job opportunities,' 'remote job opportunities.' These are just a few helpful online resources you can use to scout out jobs. Check online ESL lists on google to find the most popular companies. Sites like glassdoor.com are also beneficial where current and past employees review jobs. So you can see which companies are good and how they treat their teachers. When you've narrowed down the list for companies you're interested in, then you can start sending out your resume either on their career page, or through a recruiter online.

You will find many recruiters on facebook looking to help their company grow its teacher base. They receive a small fee for every teacher that the company hires, so they are eager to guide you through the hiring process. When you send in your resume if they like you, they will usually ask to set up an interview.

Interviewing for a teaching position online is different than other online interview processes. Most times, they will want you to prepare a demonstration/demo. These demos will determine whether you'll get you the job. They generally ask teachers to prepare a 10-minute mock class where you'll be the teacher and the interviewer will pretend to be a student. They give you a topic beforehand, something basic such as numbers, colours or facial features. This is a part of an example script of a demo class for teaching young learners at a beginner level.

Demo - Face

Hello, my name is teacher Grace. What is your name?
Hello _____, nice to meet you.
Today, we are learning about our face.

Can you say face? face, face, face
Touch your face
Very good!
Can you say eyes? Eyes, eyes, eyes
etc

By looking at this script your probably thinking there is no way you'll be able to stretch this for 10 minutes. When teaching online, the name of the game is repetition, especially with young learners. You need to repeat everything and get your students to repeat you as well. Don't forget to speak extra slowly and over enunciate. Interviewers will be looking at how you interact with your students, and they want to see you encourage your students to speak and repeat the vocabulary. During the demo you want to make clear gestures or use TPR to help your students understand your meaning. Interviewers will also be very impressed with your use of props such as a whiteboard, puppets, toys and your use of a reward system to reinforce speaking. Usually, during the demo class the "student" will make a small mistake such as mispronouncing a word, the interviewer/student will want you to see how you correct them. Youtube is an excellent tool to use to help get an idea of what to do during a demo.

After the demo, the interviewer will go over what they thought of your teaching style. Sometimes, there are a couple of rounds of interviews, and other places will have one round. So, don't worry too much. As I mentioned previously, the entire process from applying to teaching your first class may take as long as a month. After you've been offered a position, the company will start to train you on using their platform. They will give you material to read and help you to use the different functions in the classroom, so you can confidently teach a class. In my experience, I was paired with another new teacher, and together we had to practise being the teacher and the student. Finally, after you've learned the system, you will be given a schedule to teach students. Yay!

CHAPTER 4

Equipment & Rewards

Okay, so you have the job, your about to start teaching and you need to get the proper gear. I recommend not buying any new equipment until you've been teaching for a couple of months, if you can get by on used equipment, then do that first. Here is a basic list of essential equipment/ things you will need to get started teaching.

Essentials

Laptop/Computer
Stable Internet Connection
Webcam
USB Headset
Clear Backdrop
Comfy Chair (optional)
Reward System

Quiet Room/Space

The most expensive thing on this list will be the computer, so hopefully, you already have a good one. If you don't, then it might be worth it to invest in a one as you'll be working on the internet. If that's not an option for you, then any computer that is compatible with your company's platform will be fine. I suggest working on a laptop as it means you can be more portable, and take it with you when you travel, go on vacation or just want to work somewhere else for the day, If you have a desktop computer that is great as well.

Stable internet connection is another essential part of teaching online. When your teaching even though you're not physically in a classroom, you're representing the company and if teachers are continually cutting out because of internet problems you'll look unprofessional. Make sure before starting each class you keep an eye on your internet speed. There are websites such as speedtest.net that will check your internet/wifi speed. This is a great tool because you can gauge what the wifi speed for the class will be. This of course doesn't mean that your students wifi will be decent but at least it won't be your fault if the class cuts out.

You might be asked by your company to send screenshots of these wifi speed tests to prove your internet is acceptable to teach. If you live in a city where reliable wifi isn't easily available then teaching online might not be an option for you. As a new teacher, you'll be asked to prove wifi strength before teaching class.

The webcam is essential because it's how you are going to see your students and vice versa. If you have a laptop with a built-in webcam then you should be good to go. If you don't have a built-in webcam, then you need to look for one. You don't need a ridiculously expensive webcam if you only need it for teaching. Logitech generally sells good quality and low-cost webcams. You shouldn't spend more than $40 on a webcam, and you can find cheap ones at Walmart, Staples or Amazon.

You'll also need a good headset with a built-in microphone and USB port. The USB headsets tend to have good volume controls, which will be helpful during classes. I bought a Logitech headset with a USB port for $20 when I started teaching, and it still works great. Most companies will want you to have a professional-looking headset, so no apple headphones with built-in speakers.

The environment you create for your students will be very important. When you're teaching a class, your students will be able to see the space behind you. Therefore, you need to choose a smart backdrop. It wouldn't look very professional if your students could see your dirty laundry and an unmade bed. Office space would be ideal, somewhere with white walls and no background noise.

When I started teaching, I just sat on the floor in my

basement against a white wall and put a couple of lamps around me for better light as long as your students are looking at a clean, smart backdrop you're good to go.

CHAPTER 5

<u>**Classroom**</u>

Creating an engaging and memorable classroom for your students will be a big part of what distinguishes you from other teachers. Firstly you'll want to create an age appropriate space. When your teaching adults you don't want them to see cartoon characters in the background, you also don't want a blank wall. Creating the appropriate classroom space will make your students more comfortable in class. You'll also want to teach in a well lit room, teaching in a dark bedroom won't exactly encourage anyone to be taught by you again. When I teach I tend to speak louder and over enunciate, this can be quite noisy to the other people in the house so I usually teach in a basement room away from everyone. The privacy makes it easier for me to focus on teaching the lesson instead of what's happening in the next room.

Try to teach in the same place as much as possible. I know one of the best things about teaching online is that you can teach anywhere but if your background can be consistent then it will help keep your students be more focused. When I travel and teach sometimes I'll bring a couple of my background decorations and some of my reward boards, I can tape them to a white wall and it looks exactly like my regular set up at home.

Reward systems are essential for young learners to keep their attention and motivate them to speak and engage with the class. The reward systems you use don't have to be elaborate to be effective, the best ones I've seen have been very simple and easy to explain. Ice cream scoop on an ice cream cone, apple on a tree, and stars beside their names are just a couple of point systems I use to encourage student participation. Everytime a student gets a question right or tries to answer then I'll give them a reward.

I usually keep a couple of reward boards close by so I can vary it up every couple of classes. All my reward systems are cutouts I printed off the internet and glued magnets to so that I can use them on my little whiteboard. These little details are what the students will remember most. When I'm teaching group classes I'll divide my students into teams and have them work together to earn the most points. This friendly competition helps to make the classes more fun and engaging.

CHAPTER 6

<u>TPR - Total Physical Response</u>

Total physical response is a teaching method used primarily in language classes. It helps to facilitate language learning through listening and responding method. This is mostly used with young learners.

Teaching ESL is tricky because unlike other classes you don't share a common language to better explain yourself and get your point across. TPR is using exaggerated hand and body movements to better convey your meaning. When teaching you'll want to use a combination of TPR and props/pictures to teach lessons. For example if your teaching a lesson about animals and you show/draw a picture of a cat you might also use TPR to act like a cat. TPR helps us to engage our students in participating in the class, the more they interact with us the more they'll understand. Sometimes during classes our meaning is sometimes lost but TPR helps us to connect with students.

When we teach online we tend to lose that personal connection that forms between teacher and student. We have to work harder to form meaningful relationships because we're not physically with them. The more engaged students are in what your doing, the more likely they are to understand and come back.

When I was first introduced to TPR I felt really silly. I was all over the place acting out these exaggerated actions to students who were just staring blankly at me. As a teacher though you'll have to push past your insecurities to better connect with students. You might look a little silly but your students will appreciate the effort when it helps them to understand the lesson.

RESOURCES

There is a huge community of online teachers and they have been so helpful throughout my ESL career. There are so many supportive facebook groups with helpful suggestions and tips on how to deal with problems in class. Many ESL companies have their own informal facebook groups for teachers to discuss problems specific to their company. I can't tell you how many times I've had trouble with accessing my companies platform only to go to the facebook group and realize everyone has been having the same problem.

Facebook Groups

Online teaching jobs - Digital nomads teach english online

Online ESL Teachers

Digital Nomads

Youtube Tutorials

ESL Online

ESL Demo Lesson

Udemy- Online Courses

Teaching ESL Online

Online ESL - TPR in the Classroom